World Cities

PARIS

Christine Hatt

*Special photography
by Chris Fairclough*

Thameside Press

Distributed in the United States by
Smart Apple Media
1980 Lookout Drive
North Mankato, MN 56003

Printed in the USA

  Library of Congress Cataloging-in-Publication Data
Hatt, Christine.
  Paris / by Christine Hatt.
    p. cm — (World cities)
  Includes index.
  Summary: Discusses the events and people that have shaped the city
  of Paris, its history, architecture, notable sights, economy, culture,
  and way of life.
  ISBN 1-929298-30-7
    1. Paris (France)—Civilization—Juvenile literature. [1. Paris (France)]
I. Title. II. World cities (Mankato, Minn.)

DC723 .H37 2000
944'36—dc21   00-022331

9 8 7 6 5 4 3 2 1

Editor Stephanie Turnbull
Designer Helen James
Photographer Chris Fairclough
Map illustrator Lorraine Harrison
Picture researcher Kathy Lockley
Consultant Laurence Mortimore, British Council, Paris
Educational consultant Elizabeth Bassant

Additional images
AKG London: 9t, 10b, 40b, /Erich Lessing 9b, 41t; © Parc Astérix: 35t;
Bridgeman Art Library London: /Musée Carnavalet, Paris/Giraudon 36b,
/Private Collection 8b; Jean-Loup Charmet: 10t, 23b, 26t, 27b, 30t, 41bl;
Robert Harding Picture Library: 4l, 37b; Hulton Getty: 11t, 21t, 40t; Rex
Features: 20b, 24r; Roger-Viollet: /Boyer-Viollet 24l, /Collection Viollet 8t;
Frank Spooner Pictures: 11b, 12b, 13t, 38t, 38b, 39t, 41br.

Words in **bold** are explained in the glossary on pages 46 and 47.

CONTENTS

Introduction 4-5

Maps of the city 6-7

The early history of Paris 8-9

The Revolution and after. 10-11

The people of Paris 12-13

Architecture 14-15

Open spaces 16-17

Homes and housing 18-19

Education 20-21

Religion 22-23

Industry and finance 24-25

Crime and punishment 26-27

Getting around 28-29

Shops and markets 30-31

Food and drink 32-33

Entertainment 34-35

Museums and galleries 36-37

Special events 38-39

City characters 40-41

The future of Paris 42-43

Timeline 44-45

Glossary 46-47

Index 48

INTRODUCTION

Paris lies in northern France, and is the country's capital and largest city. It covers about 40 square miles on the Left and Right Banks of the Seine River and on two islands in the river. The city's population is just over two million.

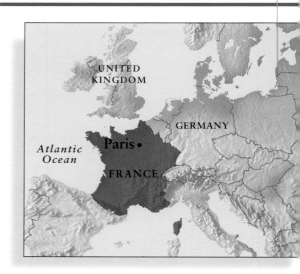

The City of Paris is enclosed by a bypass called the Boulevard Périphérique. Greater Paris, where many more people live, continues far beyond. The City, Greater Paris and the surrounding countryside make up the large Ile de France region, which has a population of over 11 million. Paris is its capital, too.

Beauty and romance

Paris is one of the world's most beautiful cities. It has many breathtaking buildings, such as Notre-Dame Cathedral and the Garnier Opera House (see pages 14-15). The elegant, tree-lined **boulevards** of the city are light and wide, and give a clear view of many landmarks. The beauty of Paris, especially in spring, makes it a favorite place to go for people in love.

▲ Two islands—the Ile de la Cité, and the smaller Ile St-Louis—stand in the middle of the Seine River. Notre-Dame Cathedral is on the Ile de la Cité.

City of Light

Over the years many great thinkers have lived in Paris. They exchanged ideas about literature and philosophy in the city's cafés and university buildings. The most famous area for intellectual conversation is the **Latin Quarter** on the Left Bank. In the eighteenth century Paris was nicknamed "City of Light" as its scholars spread the light of knowledge throughout the world.

FAST FACTS

PARIS

STATUS
Capital of France and of the Ile de France region

AREA
40 square miles

POPULATION
2.127 million (1995)

GOVERNING BODY
20 district mayors and councils;
city mayor and council

CLIMATE
Temperatures average 37°F in January
and 66°F in July

TIME ZONE
Greenwich Mean Time (GMT) plus
two hours from end March to end Oct;
GMT plus one hour from Nov to end March

CURRENCY
100 centimes = 1 French franc
(The Euro will fully replace the franc by July 2002)

OFFICIAL LANGUAGE
French

▲ The best known avenue in Paris, the Champs-Elysées, leads up to the equally famous Arc de Triomphe.

Business matters

Most French businesses and banks have their headquarters in Paris. About a quarter of French industry is based there, too, but the government wants factories to move out to new areas (see pages 24-25). Beyond Greater Paris, the Ile de France is an agricultural region, producing food for the capital's homes and restaurants.

Government in Paris

The City of Paris has a mayor and a council. They meet in the grand town hall (Hôtel de Ville). Paris is also divided into 20 districts called *arrondissements*, and each one has its own mayor and council.

Paris is the home of France's national government. It has two parts—the National Assembly, which meets in the Bourbon Palace, and the Senate, which meets in the Luxembourg Palace (see page 16). The French president lives in the grand Elysée Palace.

◄ The magnificent, nineteenth-century town hall looks out onto a square. In the past, murderers and other major criminals were executed here.

5 🌐 *Paris*

MAPS OF THE CITY

These maps show Paris as it is today. The street map gives a close-up view of the city center, while the area map shows the capital's 20 *arrondissements* (districts) and the bypass that forms its boundary. Many of the places mentioned in the book are marked.

THE PARIS ARRONDISSEMENTS

Bois de Boulogne

bypass

Bois de Vincennes

17th · 18th · 19th · 9th · 10th · 8th · 2nd · 3rd · 20th · 16th · 1st · 11th · 7th · 4th · 6th · 5th · 12th · 15th · 14th · 13th

Each Paris *arrondissement* is numbered. The first *arrondissement* is in the center of the city on the Right Bank of the Seine River. The numbering then continues outward in a spiral shape.

CENTRAL PARIS

1. La Grande Arche
2. Arc de Triomphe
3. Chaillot Palace
4. Eiffel Tower
5. Hôtel des Invalides
6. Avenue des Champs-Elysées
7. Elysée Palace
8. Tuileries Garden
9. Comédie Française
10. Louvre Museum
11. Orsay Museum
12. Delacroix Museum
13. Luxembourg Garden
14. Luxembourg Palace
15. Panthéon
16. Sorbonne
17. Latin Quarter
18. Cluny Museum
19. Ile de la Cité

20 Conciergerie	**27** Montmartre
21 Sainte-Chapelle	**28** Sacré-Coeur
22 Notre-Dame Cathedral	**29** Gare du Nord
23 Ile St-Louis	**30** Gare de l'Est
24 Hôtel de Ville	**31** St Martin's Canal
25 Pompidou Center	**32** Marais
26 Garnier Opera House	**33** Carnavalet Museum

34 Place des Vosges
35 Place de la Bastille
36 Paris Mosque
37 Botanical Garden
38 Charles de Gaulle Bridge
39 Palais d'Omnisports
40 National Library

SEINE RIVER

In the third century BC, the Parisii tribe of **Gauls** settled on an island in the Seine River that later became the Ile de la Cité. The Romans took over the island in 53 BC. They named the settlement Lutetia, and it spread to the river banks. In 212 AD Lutetia was renamed Paris, after the Parisii.

▲ A Viking raid on Paris in the ninth century AD. The Vikings repeatedly attacked Paris, killing people, looting, and burning homes.

Early rulers

A **Germanic** tribe called the Franks took over Paris and the area around it in the fifth century. Their first ruler was Clovis, who founded the **Merovingian dynasty** and the **Frankish kingdom.** He ruled from Paris, but after his death the city became less important.

A new dynasty

The Merovingian rulers grew weak and lazy. In 751 a man called Pepin the Short took over and began the **Carolingian dynasty.** Charlemagne, Pepin's son, built an empire and made Aachen, now in Germany, his capital. Paris was ruled by a governor, whose title was Count of Paris.

▲ A plague known as the Black Death swept through France from 1348 to 1349, killing about 26,000 Parisians. Victims were covered in swollen lumps.

Capetian kings

When the last Carolingian monarch died in 987, a Count of Paris called Hugh Capet became king. He made Paris his capital and it began to thrive again. This was the start of a long line of Capetian kings. During this time Notre-Dame Cathedral (see page 14) and the Louvre (see page 36) were constructed.

The Hundred Years' War

In 1328 the Capetian line of kings died out and the first **Valois** king, Philip VI, began his rule. In 1337 war broke out with England because the English king, Edward III, thought that he had the right to rule France. The war continued until 1453 and is known as the Hundred Years' War. The English took over Paris in 1420. Troops led by **Joan of Arc** failed to win the city back in 1429, but the French king Charles VII recaptured it in 1436.

▲ The 1572 massacre of Protestants began late on 23 August and went on to 24 August, St Bartholemew's Day. As a result, it is called the St Bartholemew's Day Massacre.

The Wars of Religion

Paris was a successful city during the reign of Francis I (1515-47). In 1562 the Wars of Religion began between Roman Catholics and **Huguenots**. In 1572 about 3,000 Paris Protestants were killed in a massacre. Henry IV, the first **Bourbon** king, had to become a Catholic before he was allowed into Paris in 1594, but he was later assassinated by a Catholic, in 1610.

The Sun King

In 1643 Louis XIV came to the throne. He reigned from the Palace of Versailles (see page 14) as the all-powerful Sun King, and took control of Paris government. The next king was Louis XV, who moved the court back to Paris. He was a weak man and spent far too much money on war, which plunged France into debt. The king's incompetence and new Enlightenment ideas (see page 22) made people demand a different kind of government.

◀ King Louis XIV in all his splendor. He disliked Paris, and had the Palace of Versailles built well outside the city.

THE REVOLUTION AND AFTER

Louis XVI became king in 1774. He and his wife, Marie Antoinette, lived in luxury. Meanwhile ordinary people suffered. They did not have enough food and had to pay high taxes, so they were eager for a change in the way France was run.

The French Revolution

Revolution came on July 14, 1789, when a mob stormed the Bastille prison in Paris. In 1792 the monarchy was abolished and the First **Republic** was set up. Louis XVI and Marie Antoinette were **guillotined** in 1793. The following year became known as the **Reign of Terror**, when opponents of the new government were killed.

▲ The mob that stormed the Bastille in 1789 was helped by a citizens' army called the National Guard. They used muskets and cannons to attack the prison.

Napoleon Bonaparte

Napoleon Bonaparte seized power in 1799 and was made Emperor Napoleon I in 1804. He waged war against many countries, and built the Arc de Triomphe to mark his victories of 1805. But in 1814 Britain, Russia, Austria and **Prussia** took Paris. Napoleon was finally defeated at the Battle of Waterloo in 1815.

▲ Napoleon I as painted by Jacques Louis David. Napoleon came from the island of Corsica, but he trained to be a soldier at Paris's Military School.

Napoleon III

The monarchy was restored after Napoleon's defeat, but more revolutions in 1830 and 1848 led to the setting up of the Second Republic. Napoleon's nephew, Louis-Napoleon, was elected president, but made himself Emperor Napoleon III. Together with Baron Haussmann (see page 40) he transformed Paris, constructing many fine buildings.

◄ General de Gaulle (shown in the center of this picture, wearing a cap and uniform) led the celebrations to mark the end of Nazi rule in Paris in 1944.

War and the Commune

France went to war with Prussia in 1870. Napoleon III fell from power after a defeat and the Third Republic began. Prussia conquered Paris in 1871. The French government signed a peace treaty, but many Parisians objected to this. They set up their own government, called the Commune, and took over the city. French troops violently defeated the Commune in May 1871.

The World Wars

World War I lasted from 1914 to 1918. German troops came close to Paris, but the French drove them back. In **World War II** German **Nazis** took over the city from 1940 to 1944. After this a new government was set up by General Charles de Gaulle, who had led French resistance to German rule. He resigned in 1946 and the Fourth Republic was declared.

The Fifth Republic

De Gaulle became president again in 1958 and the Fifth Republic began. In 1968 Paris students protested against the education system (see page 21) and workers went on strike. De Gaulle had to resign because of this crisis. Since then, France has had many presidents. The current leader is Jacques Chirac, who will be in power until 2002.

In 1989 Parisians ➤ celebrated the 200th anniversary of the French Revolution. People wore historical costumes, and this woman dressed as Marie Antoinette.

THE PEOPLE OF PARIS

About 20 per cent of all French people live in Paris. Many were born in the capital, but more moved to Paris to find work. The city is also home to about 350,000 foreigners, from rich business people to poor **immigrants**.

City and suburbs

Paris grew from the nineteenth century, when country people began to arrive looking for jobs in the city's new industries (see page 24). At first most of them settled in central Paris. In later years many people moved farther out, so the City population shrank. Now the growth of the **suburbs** has slowed down.

Old and young

The number of children in the City of Paris is low compared with the rest of France because many families move out to larger houses in the suburbs. The number of old people in the City, especially women, is high. About half of all Parisians live on their own.

▲ Many Paris streets are lined with fashionable cafés. Stylish, chic Parisians enjoy sitting outside and watching the world go by.

North African immigrants

About 120,000 people from the former French **colonies** of Algeria, Tunisia and Morocco live in Paris. People from these North African lands first came to the city in the 1950s, when there was a shortage of workers. Some French people protested violently against foreigners working in Paris, so an antiracist group called *SOS-Racisme* was formed.

◄ An *SOS-Racisme* march in Paris. The slogan of the group, written on the hand-shaped placard, is 'Hands off my pal'.

◄ Youssou N'Dour (far left) performing at the Bercy Arena in Paris. He sings in French, English and Wolof, a Senegalese language. He is famous in many countries.

Black Africans and Caribbeans

France also had colonies in West and Central Africa, including Senegal and Benin. Thousands of people from these countries are now Paris residents and many play a big part in the life of the city. The Senegalese singer Youssou N'Dour, for example, often works there. Paris also has a large Caribbean population, especially from places such as Martinique and Guadeloupe, as well as the former French colony of Haiti.

PARISIAN JEWS

The Jewish population of Paris grew in the late nineteenth century when refugees from Russian **pogroms** fled there. Many Jews left Paris during **World War II** because of **persecution** (see page 23). The Jewish population began to grow again in the 1950s, when many North African Jews arrived. The main Jewish Quarter of Paris is in the 4th *arrondissement*, around the Rue des Rosiers. A large number of North African Jews also live in the Belleville area.

Asian immigrants

Asians from the former French colony of **Indo-China**, which included Cambodia, Laos and part of Vietnam, make up another big foreign community in Paris. About 30,000 Asians live in the bustling Asian Quarter, or Chinatown, of the 13th *arrondissement*. The Belleville area in the 20th *arrondissement* has a large East Asian population, but is also home to Turks, Armenians and Jews (see above).

Members of the Turkish community ▲ in Paris meet at cafés like this to chat and to drink strong Turkish coffee.

ARCHITECTURE

Paris is full of fine buildings, from grand cathedrals to dazzling palaces.

Notre-Dame Cathedral

The great **Gothic** cathedral of Notre-Dame on the Ile de la Cité was built from 1163 to 1345. It was damaged in the 1789 Revolution, but restored after a campaign led by Victor Hugo (see page 40). A spire was also added. The cathedral's many features include stone **gargoyles** and three **rose windows**.

Hôtel des Invalides

The Hôtel des Invalides, a home for wounded soldiers, was built on the orders of King Louis XIV. The soldiers' houses and a hospital were completed in 1676, then two churches were added. One, in the middle of the Hôtel, is the Dôme Church, which contains the tomb of Napoleon I (see page 10). Many people come to visit this.

▲ The magnificent interior of Notre-Dame Cathedral, looking toward the high altar and the stained glass windows above.

▲ The spectacular Hôtel des Invalides. The Dôme Church, with its golden roof, was the private church of King Louis XIV.

The Palace of Versailles

Louis XIV also ordered the building of the enormous Palace of Versailles, southwest of Paris. The palace was decorated with gold to make it a fitting home for the Sun King (see page 9). Each room is richly furnished, but the most splendid and extravagant of all is the 245 foot-long Hall of Mirrors.

The Panthéon

The Panthéon was designed as a church, but it was completed in 1790 during the French Revolution, when religion was unpopular (see page 22). It was turned into a **mausoleum** instead and now contains the tombs of famous people such as scientist Marie Curie and novelists Victor Hugo and Emile Zola.

Garnier Opera House

Garnier Opera House was part of Baron Haussmann's plan for Paris (see page 10). It was designed by Charles Garnier and completed in 1875. The building is famous for its elaborate stone exterior, grand entrance hall and lush red and gold interior. The lake underneath inspired the story *The Phantom of the Opera* by Gaston Leroux.

▲ The stunning Garnier Opera House is the world's largest theater. The entrance hall, with its huge marble staircase, takes up half the building.

SEWER STORY

Beneath the graceful buildings of Paris lurk less pleasant sights. Among them are the 1,305 mile-long sewers, which were built by Baron Haussmann and which are one of his most important works. Visitors can tour through part of the sewers and go in a museum there.

The Eiffel Tower

The famous Eiffel Tower was built in 1889 to mark the centennial of the French Revolution. The 985 foot-high structure was designed by Gustave Eiffel and made from 7,000 tons of iron. There were plans to knock it down in 1909, but instead it was turned into a giant radio transmitter. About five million people visit the Eiffel Tower each year.

▼ Tourists take an elevator up the Eiffel Tower. If they are strong enough, they can climb the 1,652 steps.

Great works of Paris

In the late twentieth century, French presidents ordered a series of *grands travaux* (great works) to be constructed in Paris. As a result, striking modern buildings such as the Pompidou Center (see page 37) and the French National Library were added to the city's architecture.

OPEN SPACES

Paris did not have many parks until Napoleon III (see page 10) transformed the city. Now the capital has thousands of acres of greenery, and parks of all kinds.

▲ Toy boats sail on a pond in the Tuileries Garden. In the background is the small Carrousel Arc de Triomphe, built in 1808.

The Tuileries Garden

The Tuileries Garden, near the Louvre, was created in 1564 and redesigned in the 1990s. The garden was once part of the Tuileries Palace, which no longer exists. It has a formal, elegant layout and contains large flower beds and decorated fountains.

CITY CEMETERY

Until the late eighteenth century, there were cemeteries in central Paris. One finally became so full that it exploded, showering bones everywhere. As a result, new cemeteries had to be built outside the city center. Among them was Père Lachaise Cemetery in Belleville. The remains of many famous Paris residents are here. Among them are French singer Edith Piaf (see page 41), Irish writer Oscar Wilde and American rock star Jim Morrison.

The Luxembourg Garden

The Luxembourg Garden on the Left Bank was built in 1612. A royal palace (see page 5) was then constructed there. Many Parisians love this garden. Children can sail toy boats in the central pool, go for pony rides or visit the puppet theater. Adults can walk among the flower beds, play chess and **boules**, or learn beekeeping at the garden's hives.

Luxembourg Palace is a government building. ➤ It was once a prison, and in **World War II** it was used as the **Nazi** headquarters.

The Botanical Garden

The **Botanical Garden** on the Left Bank was set up in 1626 by two of King Louis XIII's doctors, who grew medicinal herbs there. The garden later developed into a research center containing huge greenhouses and plants from all over the world. In the eighteenth century a natural history museum and a zoo also opened in the grounds.

A shady avenue in the Botanical ▲ Garden. The park contains the oldest tree in Paris, which was brought from North America in 1635.

▲ People go to the Bois de Boulogne for its gardens, sports grounds, open-air theater and fairground rides.

Buttes-Chaumont Park

Adolphe Alphand created several parks in central Paris. They include Buttes-Chaumont Park in the northeast. The site was once a quarry, but Alphand turned it into a romantic landscape of wooded slopes. He also built a lake with an island in the middle. People climb to the Roman-style temple on top of the high island to admire the view across the city.

arisian forests

apoleon III admired London's spacious arks, and decided to create similar green aces in Paris. In 1853 he ordered engineer dolphe Alphand to transform the Bois de oulogne, an old royal hunting forest west f the city. Now the forest contains several arks and Longchamp racecourse. Alphand en worked on the Bois de Vincennes, st of the city. Paris Zoo is in this forest.

New parks

In 1992 André Citroën Park opened in the 15th *arrondissement*, on the site of an old car factory. The plants in the gardens are specially arranged to create large, bright blocks of color. The park also has a wild flower meadow. The futuristic-looking Villette Park in the northeast opened in 1993. It contains many museums (see page 37) and a cinema encased in a giant silver ball.

HOMES AND HOUSING

As the population of Paris grew, so did the number of homes. Rich people lived in grand mansions called *hôtels* in areas such as the Marais (see page 19) and the Ile St-Louis. Meanwhile poor people crowded together in old, dirty slums.

▲ Number 3, Rue Volta, is a seventeeth-century house in the style of a medieval home.

Haussmann and housing

In the nineteenth century Baron Haussmann (see page 40) demolished about 25,000 crowded, dirty Paris slums, many on the Ile de la Cité. He replaced them with stylish apartment buildings on wide boulevards. The houses were clean and well-ventilated. Thousands of Parisians still live in homes from this era.

At the front of this picture are ▼ typical nineteenth-century Parisian apartments with balconies. Behind them are modern high-rises.

Suburban slums

Many people who had lived in the slums could not afford the new apartments. They moved out of the city center into **suburbs**, especially to the east and north. Jobseekers from the countryside (see page 24) also came to the suburbs, and slums developed there. Some of these still exist today.

Rich villages

During the Haussmann era, homes for rich people were built in villages west of Paris, such as Chaillot. The villages became part of the city in 1860, when it was enlarged and divided into 20 *arrondissements*. The villages make up the 16th *arrondissement*, which is still one of the smartest areas in Paris.

THE MARAIS

In the fourteenth century the French royal family moved into the Marais area of Paris. In the seventeenth century Henry IV built the Place des Vosges there (right) and nobles built grand houses called *hôtels* nearby. When the royal court moved to Versailles, the nobles left, too, and the *hôtels* were divided into apartments. In 1962 the Marais became a conservation area and the *hôtels* were restored. Some are now museums.

High rises

After **World War II** there was a housing shortage in Paris, so large high rise projects, known as *grands ensembles*, were built outside the city. Unfortunately there were not many shops or other facilities, and residents often felt very cut-off. The projects became unpopular, and after 1965 hardly any more were built.

In the 1980s slums were cleared in the northeastern Belleville area. Many were replaced with huge apartments like this.

Plans for Paris

In 1965 a plan for the whole Paris region was drawn up. New towns were set up and development was encouraged only in certain suburbs to prevent more overcrowding in central Paris. The plan worked, and over the following years thousands of people moved out of the city center. In the outer suburbs there are many *pavillons* (detached houses) as well as apartments.

Transforming the city center

In 1967 modernization work began on homes in the center of Paris. By then, many were crumbling, and some did not even have bathrooms. At the same time many slums in the east and north were improved, or demolished and replaced with better housing. Thousands of new homes were built in the 13th *arrondissement*, in areas such as Montparnasse.

Housing today

Most Parisians now live in apartments, and rent their homes instead of buying them. Housing renovations and improvements are still going on in the city. Unfortunately these changes often lead to higher rents, driving out poorer residents.

EDUCATION

Paris has been a center of learning since the Middle Ages.
Educational standards are still high and pupils must work hard.

School system

Many French children go to nursery
from the age of three, but the official
school starting age is six. Pupils leave
primary school when they are eleven to
join a junior secondary school. At fifteen,
they begin senior secondary education
in *lycées*. Pupils are allowed to leave at
sixteen, but many stay on until eighteen.

Testing times

Pupils who stay on at school prepare for the
baccalauréat exam. They have to pass this to go
to university. Some pupils remain at their *lycées*
after the "*bac*". They work toward the entrance
examination for the *grandes écoles* (see page 21)
or study for a vocational diploma.

▲ Young school children make their way
through the streets of Paris in a long line.
They carry their books in knapsacks.

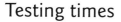

◄ Students attending
a lecture at the
Sorbonne. Above
them is a statue of
the seventeenth-
century philosopher,
mathematician and
physicist Blaise Pascal.

The University of Paris

In 1208 the University of
Paris was set up in the **Latin
Quarter**. Many individual colleges
were then created, including the
Sorbonne in 1253. The Sorbonne
was closed during the Revolution,
but became the center of the
University of Paris in 1821.
In the following years, many
famous professors taught there,
for example, the well-known
scientists Pierre and Marie Curie.

tudent protests

he University of Paris is now divided nto 13 universities. This split was made in 1968, when Paris students rotested against overcrowding, oor teaching, the government and world politics. Rioting began and nrest spread among workers as well as students. The government ad to make changes to the education ystem to stop the protests.

▲ A violent clash between angry Parisian students and the riot police (see page 26) in June 1968.

Top-class training

The top centers of higher education in Paris are the *grandes écoles*. Among the most famous is the Ecole Polytechnique, which trains engineers. It was based in the Latin Quarter until 1977, when it moved to the **suburbs**. The Ecole Normale Supérieure is on the Left Bank. It prepares students to be teachers at *lycées* or universities.

THE PASTEUR INSTITUTE

The Pasteur Institute opened in Paris in 1888. Its aim was to continue the medical research work of its first director, Louis Pasteur (see page 41). Experts at the institute have since developed a cure for **diphtheria** and a vaccine against **tuberculosis**. Now they are trying to find treatments and cures for new diseases such as AIDS.

▲ The French Institute, home of the 40 members of the French Academy. They try to prevent the use of English words (such as "jogging") in French.

The French Institute

In 1795 five academic societies joined to form the French Institute. The main role of one of its societies, the French Academy, is to protect the French language. The Institute is located in a seventeenth-century building on the Right Bank.

RELIGION

A Ancient Romans worshiped many gods in Paris. Christianity came to the city in the third century, and remains the religion of most modern-day Parisians.

Catholics and Protestants

Once Christianity took root, many Catholic churches were built in Paris. They include Notre-Dame Cathedral (see page 14) and the thirteenth-century Sainte-Chapelle nearby. In the sixteenth century the Wars of Religion broke out between Catholics and Protestants (see page 9). In 1685 Louis XIV expelled the Protestant **Huguenots**, who fled abroad.

Enlightenment and Revolution

A movement known as the Enlightenment grew in Europe in the eighteenth century. Its supporters, such as the writer Voltaire, did not agree with religion and government. They wanted a society based on reason and science. Their ideas inspired leaders of the Revolution, who closed many Paris churches and turned others, including Notre-Dame, into Temples of Reason.

▲ Sainte-Chapelle was divided into two parts, the upper chapel (above) for royalty and the lower chapel for servants.

◄ Sacré-Coeur Church was built after the Franco-Prussian War (see page 11) by Catholics, as a token of thanks to God that Paris was not totally destroyed.

Catholicism today

In 1801 Napoleon I restored Catholicism in France, but antichurch feeling remained strong. Most Parisians now are Catholics, but only a few worship regularly. The city contains many Catholic churches, such as the white, domed Sacré-Coeur in Montmartre, completed in 1914

Muslims in Paris

Most of the North Africans in Paris are Muslims, so the city has many Muslim places of worship, called mosques. They include the Paris Mosque in the **Latin Quarter**. It opened in 1926 and has a courtyard decorated with mosaic tiles, as well as a large prayer hall. Nearby is the modern Arab World Institute. This aims to improve relations between Western and Arab cultures.

The Paris Mosque is used every day ➤ by the city's Muslims. Its central tower, or minaret, is almost 108 feet high.

The Jewish community

Jews have lived in Paris since the Middle Ages. They were persecuted by the **Nazis** in **World War II**, and thousands were sent to **concentration camps**. A memorial to the dead now stands on the Ile de la Cité. About 350,000 Jews now live in Greater Paris. Places of worship in the Jewish Quarter include the **Art Nouveau** Guimard Synagogue.

Buddhism

The main Buddhist temple in Paris stands in the Bois de Vincennes (see page 17), on the edge of Daumesnil Lake. The impressive, Tibetan-style structure contains a huge statue of the Buddha.

THE DREYFUS AFFAIR

In the late nineteenth century, a French Jew called Alfred Dreyfus joined the army and studied engineering at the Ecole Polytechnique in Paris (see page 21). Later he was convicted of spying, thrown out of the army (left) and sentenced to life imprisonment. His family fought to prove his innocence, and demonstrations for and against him were held on the Paris streets. Many people opposed Dreyfus because he was a Jew, which showed the high level of **anti-Semitism** in France. Others, including the novelist Emile Zola, supported him. In 1906 Dreyfus was found to be innocent.

INDUSTRY AND FINANCE

The **Industrial Revolution** arrived in Paris in the nineteenth century and changed the city dramatically. Now the capital's main strengths are business and finance.

An industrialized city

By 1848 there were 65,000 industries in Paris. Thousands of people came to the city to find work, and the population rose to over one million. Railroad and canal networks also grew (see pages 28-29). Soon it was easy to transport coal and other raw materials to Paris, so industries such as engineering developed.

▲ Assembly-line workers putting together sturdy Renault cars in 1931. Nowadays there are hardly any car factories in Paris.

FRENCH FASHIONS

Paris is the world capital of the fashion industry. An Englishman called Charles Frederick Worth was the first person to set up a Paris fashion house, in 1845. Great French designers followed, such as Coco Chanel and Christian Dior. The highlights of the fashion industry year are the January and July catwalk shows. Many are held in the Louvre. The creations below are by John Galliano, an English designer who works in Paris.

Growth and change

Paris industry grew for many years. Factories spread into the **suburbs** and produced everything from bicycles to chemicals. Later, companies such as Citroën began to make cars. But growth slowed in the 1930s when **depression** hit Paris. The situation became even worse during **World War II**, when the city was controlled by German troops.

▲ La Grande Arche is an enormous hollow cube. Inside the arch is a conference center and an exhibition area.

Renewal and relocation

In the 1950s, after the war, the government made a big effort to renew industry and to spread jobs evenly across France. It paid grants-in-aid to firms that set up outside Paris, so many car manufacturers and other companies moved out of the city.

Industry today

Paris has lost thousands of industrial jobs since the 1960s, but it still has about 25 per cent of the French total. Some of these jobs are in fashion (see box), publishing, computing and electronics. The tourist industry is also growing. It was boosted when Disneyland Paris opened in the new town of Marne-La-Vallée in 1992.

Building business

The French government wants business in Paris to expand, especially in certain suburbs (see page 19). These include La Défense, a western district that contains the skyscraper offices of many large, important companies. A spectacular building called La Grande Arche was added in 1989.

Financial center

Paris is the largest financial center in France. The Bank of France was set up by Napoleon I and is one of the most important financial buildings in the city. It stands in the 2nd *arrondissement*. Near the Bank of France is the Stock Exchange, which is the third largest in Europe, after London and Frankfurt.

Paris is already ► prepared for the full introduction of the Euro in 2002 (see page 5). This café menu gives prices in Euros as well as francs.

CRIME AND PUNISHMENT

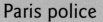 There was a lot of crime in early Paris. The busy streets were full of pickpockets, cutthroats and beggars who pretended to be sick or injured. Captured criminals were thrown into grim prisons such as the Châtelet and the Bastille. Law and order were established over the years and nowadays the city is fairly safe.

Paris police

The first major Paris police force was set up in the seventeenth century. Today there are several forces. **Gendarmes** deal with serious crimes. Local crime is dealt with by the Police Nationale. This force has a section called the CRS, which is responsible for riot control. All French police carry guns.

Police museum

Anyone interested in the history of the Paris police can visit a small museum in the **Latin Quarter**. It contains some of the terrifying weapons used by criminals of the past, as well as arrest warrants for such leaders of the French Revolution as Georges Danton.

◄ Two members of the Police Nationale patrol the streets of Paris. Their headquarters is on the Ile de la Cité.

City crime

Like all big cities, Paris has many pickpockets. They gather in crowded tourist areas such as Montmartre and skillfully steal money, credit cards and other valuables from unwary foreigners. Violent crime in Paris is rare, but some places are dangerous at night, especially large parks such as the Bois de Boulogne.

The Conciergerie, by the Seine River. ➤ Its tower contains a fourteenth-century clock, the oldest in Paris.

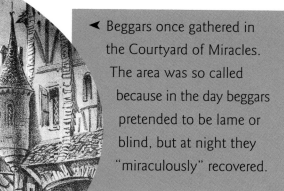

◄ Beggars once gathered in the Courtyard of Miracles. The area was so called because in the day beggars pretended to be lame or blind, but at night they "miraculously" recovered.

Paris prisons

The infamous Bastille Prison was burned down in 1790, a year after the Revolution began there (see page 10). The Châtelet Prison was destroyed in the nineteenth century. One old Paris prison remains—the Conciergerie on the Ile de la Cité. It was once part of a palace, but during the **Reign of Terror** prisoners were held and tortured there. Marie Antoinette's cell has now been reconstructed and visitors can go into it.

Laying down the law

Napoleon I reorganized French law. The new laws that he created are known as the *Code Napoléon* and are still used in France. The Paris law courts are in a large block of buildings called the Palace of Justice. It stands on the Ile de la Cité. Visitors are allowed to sit in on trials or to watch lawyers meeting clients in the seventeenth-century lobby.

THE MAN IN THE IRON MASK

In 1698, during the reign of Louis XIV, a mysterious prisoner wearing a black velvet mask arrived at the Bastille Prison. Voltaire (see page 22), who was also a prisoner there, thought that the man was the king's **illegitimate** older brother. Other people believed that he was the king's illegitimate son, or a finance minister called Nicolas Fouquet, who had been fired for corruption. The prisoner died at the Bastille in 1703. Alexandre Dumas later wrote a novel based on this called *The Man in the Iron Mask*. The prisoner's true identity remains a mystery.

GETTING AROUND

Paris is a busy place, and there are many traffic jams on the roads. The best way to travel is by public transportation. Buses and subways are quick, cheap and efficient.

▲ The Métro is a quick way to get around Paris. Many station entrances are decorated in the **Art Nouveau** style, as shown here.

Métro and RER

The subway in the City of Paris is called the Métropolitain—Métro for short. Its first line opened in 1900 and by 1935 there were 13 lines. A fourteenth line, the Météor, opened in 1998. As well as the Métro, Paris has the RER network of high-speed trains. These trains travel far into the **suburbs**.

Riding by rail

Paris's first large railroad stations, the Gare de l'Est and the Gare du Nord, were built in the nineteenth century. Now the city has six major stations, each serving a different part of France. Passengers can also take a train from Paris to other European countries. Fast TGVs travel on many routes in France, as well as to Amsterdam and Brussels. Eurostar trains to London through the Channel Tunnel leave from the Gare du Nord.

Bus travel

The first successful Paris bus service began in 1828 and used horse-drawn vehicles. Now there are hundreds of bus routes across the city. Buses run all day and most of the night. Passengers pay by stamping their tickets in a machine on board.

A sleek TGV (*Train à Grande Vitesse*, or ➤ High-Speed Train) at the Gare du Nord. These trains travel at up to 186 mph.

On the water

Pleasure boats known as *bateaux-mouches* travel up and down the Seine, giving tourists a fine view of the waterside sights. Barges also use the river to carry goods to the Channel port of Le Havre. The city has a network of canals, too, including St Martin's Canal. Boats on the canal take passengers on trips through many beautiful areas of Paris.

▲ Pleasure boats cruise regularly up and down the Seine River. Large *bateaux-mouches* carry up to 400 passengers. *Bateaux-vedettes* (above) are smaller versions.

On the road

Traffic congestion in Paris has grown worse as the number of cars on the road has increased. Old roads have been widened and new roads have been built, but the problem remains. Traffic flow improved when the Boulevard Périphérique around the city opened in 1973, but this, too, soon became jammed with traffic. Paris authorities are still looking for a solution.

CYCLING LANES

As part of the campaign to make getting around Paris easier, about 62 miles of bicycle lanes have been built. The lanes have traffic lights at handlebar level which are easy for cyclists to see. But cycling in Paris can be very dangerous as motorists often drive in the bicycle lanes.

A funicular (cable car) ➤ railroad travels up the steep hill to the Sacré-Coeur church in Montmartre. This railroad is popular with tourists who cannot face the climb.

ir travel

ris has two main airports. The largest is Charles de aulle Airport, to the north. This is used for international ghts. Orly Airport, to the south, is used for shorter ternational journeys and for flights within France.

SHOPS AND MARKETS

Paris shops have it all—designer clothes, fine foods, rare books and more. People can browse as well as buy at the city's many markets.

Department stores

The first Paris department store was Au Bon Marché, which opened on the Left Bank in 1852. Another long-established store is La Samaritaine. It opened in 1896 in an impressive cast-iron building on the Right Bank, and since then has spread to fill three neighboring buildings too. Other famous department stores in Paris are Galeries Lafayette and Printemps.

The Forum des Halles

In 1969 Paris's huge wholesale food market, Les Halles, moved out of the City to a southern **suburb**. A modern glass shopping complex called Forum des Halles was built on the market's old site. It has four levels and contains many shops and restaurants, as well as a swimming pool.

▲ This picture from 1875 shows the busy shop floors and staircase of Au Bon Marché, then the largest department store in the world.

▲ The Passage des Panoramas arcade opened in 1800. One engraver's shop there is still decorated exactly as it was in 1840.

Shopping arcades

Paris has about 20 covered **arcades** full of small, specialty shops. The oldest is the Passage du Caire, which opened in 1798. It is decorated with statues of an Ancient Egyptian goddess. The nineteenth-century Passage Jouffroy is full of collectable toys.

Fashion boutiques

The richest Parisians have clothes made for them at fashion houses. Slightly less wealthy shoppers buy designer clothes in boutiques. Most of these chic shops are in the Rue du Faubourg-St-Honoré and the fashionable area between the Arc de Triomphe and the Seine.

uying books

aris has many bookshops, but one of the most famous no longer exists. It was called hakespeare and Company and was opened y an American woman in 1919. James Joyce nd other writers often met there. The store as closed down by the **Nazis** in 1941.

▲ Book, picture and souvenir stalls line the quays along the Seine River, especially on the Left Bank. Many tourists come here.

Paris markets

One Paris market is specially for book-lovers. It takes place at weekends on the Rue Brancion, and some items for sale are valuable antiques. The city also has many **flea markets**. The largest is Saint Ouen, which has more than 2,000 stalls. The Ile de la Cité flower market is the oldest in Paris, dating back to 1808. On Sundays a bird market is held on the same site.

MONTMARTRE

The northern, villagelike quarter of Montmartre is a popular tourist place. Most people go there to visit the Sacré-Coeur church (see page 22), but there are many other attractions. These include the St Pierre market and nearby shops, which sell beautiful fabrics, and the Place du Tertre. This is full of souvenir shops, as well as portrait painters eager to make speedy sketches of passersby—for a fee.

Fine foods

One of the best food stores in Paris is Fauchon on Place de la Madeleine. It sells more than 20,000 foods in six departments. Specialty food shops include La Maison du Chocolat, which sells handmade chocolates, and Maison de la Truffe, the place to buy expensive **truffles**.

◄ A high-class Parisian food store specializing in *charcuterie*. This is the name given to all sorts of cold meats.

FOOD AND DRINK

Many people think that French food is the best in the world, and there is nowhere better to try it than Paris. The city's restaurants sell everything from top-class *haute cuisine* (see page 33) to fast food with French flair. At home, Parisians love to prepare and enjoy food and wine.

▲ A spectacular display of crabs, oysters and other seafood outside a restaurant, designed to tempt customers in.

Everyday meals

Parisians often eat croissants or crusty bread and jam for breakfast, with a big bowl of coffee or hot chocolate. Lunch used to be the main meal of the day and took two or more hours to eat. But in modern Paris, a quick **baguette** sandwich is more common, except at weekends. When they have time, many families share a four-course evening meal consisting of an appetiser, a fish or meat dish, cheese and a dessert.

Restaurants

Eating out first became popular in Paris during the 1820s, when many fine restaurants opened. Now the city has over 8,000 eating places. Customers can order a fixed price meal or choose dishes from a wider, more expensive menu. This is known as eating *à la carte*.

CAFE CULTURE

Paris cafés serve breakfast in the morning, then snacks, coffee, wine and beer all day. Over the years many famous people have met in the cafés of the Left Bank. In the early twentieth century, Russian revolutionary leader Vladimir Lenin drank at La Rotonde in Montparnasse. In the 1930s, the American writer Ernest Hemingway spent a lot of time at Les Deux Magots café in St Germain (left). This café became popular in the 1940s with **Existentialists**, such as writer Jean-Paul Sartre. The café is now a tourist attraction.

Top-quality cooking

The finest French cooking is known as *haute cuisine,* which involves preparing elaborate, five-course meals. One of the top *haute cuisine* restaurants in Paris is called Alain Ducasse, named after the chef who cooks there. Another favorite is called Le Grand Véfour. Its former customers include Napoleon I.

Bistros and brasseries

Bistros are simple restaurants that serve basic French food, for example, broiled meats. Many are family-run, but in Paris there are also bistro chains. Brasseries are usually larger and serve food all day until late at night. They also have a range of beers and wines. La Coupole brasserie is the most famous in the city, and many stars have dined there.

A falafel store in ➤ the Rue des Roisiers (see page 13), the heart of Paris's main Jewish district. The shop sign is in Hebrew as well as French.

▲ In the 1930s, members of the Lapin Agile **cabaret** in Montmartre planted vines on the hillside nearby. This vineyard still exists.

Foreign food

Not all eating places in Paris are French. Senegalese restaurants serve dishes such as beef in peanut sauce, while Moroccan restaurants specialize in **tagines**. Vietnamese and Chinese restaurants offer a range of rice and noodle-based meals. A popular street food sold in the Jewish Quarter is falafel, which are chick-pea balls.

Paris wine

Parisians drink wine, often French wine, with most meals. The city is not an important wine-growing area, but it does have a few vineyards in Montmartre.

ENTERTAINMENT

In the Middle Ages Paris was famous for its street fairs, where jugglers, actors and musicians amused the crowds. Modern-day entertainment can be found at theaters and sports grounds.

▲ The present Comédie Française theater. In the entrance hall is a chair on which the playwright Molière collapsed in 1673 while acting at the old Comédie Française.

Paris theater

Paris has more than 100 theaters that stage many types of shows. The Comédie Française theater specializes in plays by classical French dramatists such as Molière. The theater was founded in 1680 by Louis XIV, but it is now in an eighteenth-century building. The Odéon Theater shows many foreign-language plays. Café-theaters such as Point Virgule put on light entertainment, including sketches and songs.

Movie culture

The first ever movie was shown in Paris in 1895. It was set up by the Lumière brothers, inventors of the **cinematograph**. Parisians have been passionate movie-goers ever since, and their city now has over 350 screens. There are IMAX theaters at Villette Park and La Défense.

Classical music

Classical music halls include the Champs-Elysées Theater, where the French National Orchestra plays, and Music City in Villette Park. Concerts take place in Notre-Dame and other churches. Opera is performed at the Garnier and Bastille Opera Houses.

◀ One of the many multiscreen theaters on the Champs-Elysées. There are often long lines for tickets.

Theme parks

Disneyland (see page 25) is the best known Paris theme park. It has five areas, including Fantasyland, where visitors meet Snow White. Many French children love Parc Astérix, in the Plailly **suburb**. There they can take part in the action-packed adventures of Astérix the **Gaul**, the famous comic strip character.

▲ Parents and children on a visit to Parc Astérix mingle with characters including Astérix himself (far left).

Sporting scene

All kinds of sports are played in Paris. The Palais d'Omnisports indoor arena opened in 1984. Major events held there include show jumping and tennis. Rugby and soccer are often played at the Parc des Princes, but the largest soccer field in Paris is the 80,000-seat French Stadium, built for the 1998 World Cup. Top-class tennis matches and horse racing take place in the Bois de Boulogne (see pages 38-39).

Rock, pop and jazz

All kinds of music can be heard at Music City in Villette Park, especially traditional songs from other countries. The nearby Zénith Theater is one of the main pop spots in Paris. Others include La Cigale, which is a former theater in Montmartre. Jazz lovers can hear their favorite musicians at nightspots such as Duc des Lombards and Le Sunset.

CABARETS

In the nineteenth century, many **cabarets** opened in the Montmartre area. They included the Moulin Rouge (left), where women performed a high-kicking dance called the can-can. It became especially famous after artist Henri Toulouse-Lautrec drew the dancers on advertising posters. The Moulin Rouge is still a nightclub, along with similar places such as the Folies Bergère. Their audiences are mainly tourists, not Parisians.

MUSEUMS AND GALLERIES

Paris has more than 100 museums and art galleries, from the long-established Louvre to modern buildings such as Science City.

◀ The old Louvre palace and the new glass pyramid, which was designed by Chinese-American architect IM Pei, stand side by side. Some people think that the pyramid looks completely out of place.

The Louvre Museum

The Louvre was once a magnificent royal palace. It became a museum in 1793. In the twentieth century the Louvre was modernized and a large glass pyramid was built in the courtyard. Visitors enter the museum through a corridor underneath the pyramid. Exhibits include the *Mona Lisa* painting by Leonardo da Vinci and ancient Egyptian, Greek and Roman remains.

History museums

The Carnavalet Museum tells the history of Paris. Exhibits include a model **guillotine**. The Cluny Museum in the **Latin Quarter** has a fine collection of medieval arts and crafts, as well as the remains of Paris's Roman baths.

The Orsay Museum

The Orsay Museum opened in 1986. It is housed in a beautiful old railroad station that dates from 1900. The museum displays art produced between 1848 and 1914, filling the gap between the older paintings in the Louvre and those in the Museum of Modern Art. Many of its exhibits are by **Impressionist** artists such as Claude Monet.

The model guillotine from the Carnavalet Museum. The French first used this method of execution in 1792, during the Revolution.

The Pompidou Center

The Pompidou Center opened in 1977 and shocked many people with its bold design. The huge glass and plastic building, designed by architects Richard Rogers and Renzo Piano, has all the pipes, cables, lifts and escalators on the outside. Inside is the National Museum of Modern Art, which contains paintings by Pablo Picasso, Henri Matisse and many others. The center is now being renovated (see page 42).

▲ The Pompidou Center is named after Georges Pompidou, French president from 1969 to 1974.

Science City

The giant glass and steel Science City in Villette Park provides fun for visitors of all ages. Its displays cover all sorts of scientific topics, from how volcanoes work to the secrets of the sea. There are interactive exhibits, computerized games and a flight simulator. The museum also has a planetarium, where images of the stars and planets are projected onto the ceiling.

Objects on display at Science City include a ▼ jet fighter and a high-speed train. About five million people visit the museum every year.

CHAILLOT PALACE

Chaillot Palace is a huge building containing four museums. The Museum of Mankind tells the story of human evolution and of the world's different peoples. The Marine Museum is all about the French navy. The Museum of French Monuments displays sculptures from many eras of history, while the Cinema Museum is filled with inventions from the world of filmmaking. The Palace also has theaters for plays and movies.

House museums

The former homes of some famous Paris residents are now museums. The nineteenth-century artist Eugène Delacroix lived in St Germain for several years, and his house is now a museum of his life. Delacroix painted events such as the French Revolution.

SPECIAL EVENTS

Most Parisians leave Paris in August for their annual summer vacation, but for the rest of the year the city is buzzing with activity.

New Year festivities

The New Year arrives noisily in the French capital when a grand parade makes its way through Montmartre on January 1. A few weeks later, the Asian Quarter in the 13th *arrondissement* (see page 13) erupts with dragon dances and other celebrations for Chinese New Year.

Paris in April

The trees of Paris blossom in April, which is the traditional time for romantic couples to visit the city. The Paris International Marathon is also held in this month. The route runs from the Place de la Concorde to Avenue Foch, near the Arc de Triomphe.

▲ The Waiters' Race is in June. Runners have to balance a bottle and glasses on their tray.

Spring events

A special event is held at the Palace of Versailles on Sundays from early May to early October. This is the Grandes Eaux Musicales show, during which music plays as the palace's 32 fountains and pools are illuminated. In late May and early June, the French Open Tennis Championships are held at the Roland Garros Stadium in the Bois de Boulogne.

◄ A dazzling display of fireworks always lights up central Paris on the evening of Bastille Day, July 14.

NATURE WATCH

Kestrels nest in the towers of Notre-Dame Cathedral and their chicks usually hatch in May. The young birds are ready to make their first flights in July, so every year birdwatchers set up cameras, videos and telescopes nearby. Passersby can also observe the chicks' early efforts to soar high above the city streets.

Summer celebrations

The greatest event of the Paris year is Bastille Day on July 14. It commemorates the start of the French Revolution, when the populace stormed the Bastille Prison (see page 10). During the day the French armed forces and fire brigades parade down the Champs-Elysées. Spectacular fireworks round off the celebrations in the evening. Later in July the Champs-Elysées welcomes cyclists finishing the Tour de France race.

▲ The Prix de l'Arc de Triomphe in October is a popular event for fashionable and wealthy Parisians.

Autumn events

Paris hosts an Autumn Festival of theater, music and dance. It runs from mid-September to December and there are performances in many places. On the first Saturday in October, a festival to celebrate the grape harvest is held in Montmartre (see page 33). Then on the first Sunday in October the Prix de l'Arc de Triomphe takes place. This famous horserace is run at Longchamp in the Bois de Boulogne (see page 17).

▼ The glittering Galeries Lafayette department store during the Christmas season. A huge, brightly lit tree is the centerpiece of the display.

In the winter

As Christmas nears, Parisians brighten their streets with lights and decorations. On December 24 many people go to Midnight Mass in Notre-Dame Cathedral and other churches, then make their way home in the early hours of Christmas morning.

Over the centuries people of almost every profession, from writers to politicians, have been proud to live in Paris. Here you can read about some of the city's most celebrated occupants.

▲ Victor Hugo wrote many poems plays and novels, including the story *Les Misérables* (1862)

Victor Hugo

Victor Hugo was a nineteenth-century writer who served as a member of the National Assembly and Senate in Paris. His book *The Hunchback of Notre-Dame* (1831) inspired the restoration of Notre-Dame cathedral. Hugo's writing and campaigns against injustice made him a hero. When he died 500,000 people lined the streets of Paris to mourn him.

Baron Haussmann

Georges Eugène Haussmann was born in the Alsace region of France in 1809. He trained to be a lawyer in Paris, where the crowded, dirty slums filled him with dismay. In 1853 Haussmann was made responsible for modernizing the city. Building and demolition work continued for 16 years. The total cost of the new Paris that Haussmann created was about $34 billion.

◄ Baron Haussmann was the Prefect of the Seine, the top administrative official in Paris, from 1853 to 1870. His plans transformed the city.

SAINT GENEVIEVE

The **patron saint** of Paris is Geneviève. She was a nun in the fifth century AD, when the Roman Empire was under attack from tribes. In 451 troops led by Attila the Hun were heading for Paris. Geneviève urged the people of the city to pray for help. According to legend, she then had a vision in which Attila turned away from Paris. He really did so, and the amazed Parisians believed that Geneviève's prayers had saved them.

Louis Pasteur

Louis Pasteur studied at the Ecole Normale Supérieure in Paris. In 1857 he became its Director of Scientific Studies. Pasteur was a brilliant research scientist who invented **pasteurization** and a **rabies** vaccine. In 1888 the Pasteur Institute was set up (see page 21). Pasteur was its director until his death in 1895. He was buried in a grand tomb underneath the Institute.

▲ Louis Pasteur at work in his laboratory. It has been exactly reconstructed in a museum that is part of the Pasteur Institute.

Edith Piaf

Edith Piaf, real name Edith Gassion, was born in Belleville, Paris in 1915. She left home as a teenager and earned money by singing. In 1935 the agent Louis Leplée heard her beautiful voice and launched her career. He nicknamed her "*la môme piaf*" (the urchin sparrow). Edith Piaf's songs, such as *La Vie en Rose*, brought her success, but her life was tragic. She died in 1963 and was buried in Père Lachaise cemetery.

This picture shows Edith Piaf in front ▲ of the music for *La Vie en Rose*, a love song that she made famous.

Jacques Chirac

Jacques Chirac is a famous **right-wing** politician who was born in Paris. In 1977 he became the first mayor of the city since 1871, when the position was banned after the Commune uprising (see page 11). Jacques Chirac was twice Prime Minister of France in the 1970s and 1980s, and in 1995 became the country's President.

Jacques Chirac studied ➤ at a Parisian *grande école* (see page 21) that trains people to be high-powered government officials and politicians.

THE FUTURE OF PARIS

Paris is at the heart of French life—its politics, business, education and culture. Both Paris and France as a whole are changing to meet the needs of life in the new millennium.

▲ The architect Patrick Berger created the Arts Viaduct. The arches once supported the main railroad line from Paris to Strasbourg, in northern France.

Industry and business

Since the 1950s the French government has encouraged industries to set up outside Paris (see page 25). This policy will probably continue. The government also wants Paris to become a stronger financial center so that it can play a big role in the **European Union**.

Developing areas

A lot of redevelopment work is taking place in Paris. Buildings such as the Palais d'Omnisports and the National Library are part of a plan to improve the poor eastern half of the city. Another developing area is Reuilly, slightly farther north. Here old railroad arches are now the Arts Viaduct, a collection of shops selling crafts such as tapestries, sculpture and jewelry.

▲ The old railroad track above the Arts Viaduct is now part of the Planted Promenade that runs from central Paris to the Bois de Vincennes.

Renovation work

Many Paris buildings are being renovated at the moment, including the Pompidou Center (see page 37). One of the original architects, Renzo Piano, is working on the project. Renovation is also under way at the Louvre and at two of the museums in Chaillot Palace.

River renewal

Changes are taking place on and around the Seine River, too. Gardeners are replanting the banks and creating more paths for walkers. A new bridge named after Charles de Gaulle (see page 11) has opened in the east to provide easy access to Austerlitz station from the Right Bank. The Alma Bridge, near where Diana, Princess of Wales died in 1997, is now a tourist site.

(see page 11)

A PATH THROUGH PARIS

Time around the world is measured from a line of longitude that passes through Greenwich in London. But until 1911, the French measured time from a line that passed through Paris. Now French people are planting trees and building a path all along this line. On July 14, 2000 a huge picnic will be held there to celebrate the first Bastille Day anniversary of the new millennium.

Behind the scaffolding, workers ▲ are busy repairing and reshaping the embankments of the Seine.

Transportation news

The new Météor underground line (see page 28) is part of the plan to ease the traffic problems in Paris. The government also aims to build more cycle lanes throughout the city, but this will probably not be enough to persuade thousands of Parisians to abandon their cars.

(see page 28)

...lections 2002

...ench presidents serve for seven years. ...cques Chirac (see page 41) took office ...1995, so elections are due in 2002. ...hirac will probably stand again, but he ...ill face strong opposition from **left-wing** ...d **Green** candidates. The future for ...ris and France is, as always, uncertain.

(see page 41)

The new Charles de Gaulle Bridge on ▲ the east side of Paris is one of 37 bridges that cross the Seine in the city.

TIMELINE

 This timeline shows some of the most important dates in the history of Paris. All the events are mentioned earlier in the book.

BC

Third century
Gauls *settle on an island in the Seine River*

53
Romans take over the island

THIRD CENTURY AD

212
City is named Paris, after the Parisii

FIFTH CENTURY

*Franks take over Paris and found
the* **Merovingian dynasty**

EIGHTH CENTURY

751
Carolingian *dynasty founded*

TENTH CENTURY

987
*Hugh Capet becomes king; Capetian
dynasty begins*

TWELFTH CENTURY

1163 -1345
Notre-Dame Cathedral constructed

THIRTEENTH CENTURY

1208
University of Paris founded

1253
Sorbonne founded

FOURTEENTH CENTURY

1328
Valois *dynasty begins*

1337-1453
*Hundred Years' War between
France and England*

SIXTEENTH CENTURY

1562
Wars of Religion begin

1572
St Bartholomew's Day Massacre

1589
Bourbon *dynasty begins*

SEVENTEENTH CENTURY

1643-1715
Reign of Louis XIV, the Sun King

1676
Most of the Hôtel des Invalides completed

1685
Huguenots *expelled from France*

EIGHTEENTH CENTURY

1789
French Revolution; Bastille Prison stormed

1792
Monarchy abolished

1793-1794
Reign of Terror

1799
Napoleon Bonaparte seizes power

NINETEENTH CENTURY

1804
Napoleon Bonaparte becomes
Emperor Napoleon I

1805
Arc de Triomphe built

1814
Paris taken over by Britain, Russia,
*Austria and **Prussia***

1815
Napoleon I defeated at Battle of Waterloo

1830
Second revolution in France

1848
Third revolution leads to Second Republic;
Napoleon I's nephew becomes president

1852
President makes himself Napoleon III

1853-1869
Baron Haussmann rebuilds city

1870
War begins between France and Prussia
Third Republic declared

1871
Paris taken over and France defeated
Establishment and defeat of Paris Commune

1889
Eiffel Tower constructed

TWENTIETH CENTURY

1900
First Paris Métro line opens

1914
Sacré-Coeur church completed

1914-1918
***World War I;** France and others*
defeat Germany

1930s
*Economic **depression** hits Paris*

1940-1944
*Paris occupied by **Nazis** during*
World War II

1944
General Charles de Gaulle returns from
London to set up a French government

1946
De Gaulle resigns; Fourth Republic declared

1958
De Gaulle returns to power;
Fifth Republic begins

1968
Violent protests by students and workers

1977
Jacques Chirac becomes first mayor
of Paris since 1871

1986
Orsay Museum opens

1992
Disneyland Paris opens

1995
Jacques Chirac becomes French president

TWENTY-FIRST CENTURY

2002
Next presidential elections due
Euro will fully replace the franc as currency

GLOSSARY

anti-Semitism   Prejudice against and persecution of Jews.

arcade   A covered passageway with shops on both sides. The shops are sometimes set into arches.

Art Nouveau   A style of art and architecture that was popular from about 1890 to 1910. It featured swirling shapes and images of natural objects such as leaves.

baguette   A long, thin loaf of crusty bread.

botanical garden   A garden where plants are studied by scientists as well as grown for public enjoyment.

boules   A French game in which people roll metal balls along the ground in an attempt to hit a smaller ball.

boulevard   A wide road, often tree lined.

Bourbon   Of or relating to the royal dynasty that ruled France from 1589 to 1793 and from 1815 to 1848.

cabaret   A stage show with singing and dancing acts.

Carolingian   Of or relating to the royal dynasty that ruled France from 751 to 987 AD.

cinematograph   A combined movie camera and projector.

colony   A country that is ruled by another country.

concentration camp   A place where large numbers of people are held prisoner. The Nazis set up many concentration camps where they killed more than six million people, most of them Jews.

depression   A time of low business growth and high unemployment.

diphtheria   A serious, infectious disease that causes fever and makes breathing difficult.

dynasty   A family that rules a country for generations.

European Union (EU)   An alliance of 15 European countries, including France and the UK. The union was set up to improve trade. The countries also work together on political matters such as foreign policy.

Existentialist   A person who accepts the ideas of Existentialism. This teaches that life is meaningless, and that only personal experiences and actions, not fixed religious or other beliefs, are important.

flea market   A market that sells a wide variety of cheap, and often secondhand, goods.

Frankish Kingdom   The kingdom set up by Clovis, ruler of a Germanic tribe called the Franks, in about 500 AD. The Frankish Kingdom spread across Europe, but in 843 it was split into three parts. The western part eventually developed into modern France.

gargoyle   A carving of an ugly human or animal face. Gargoyles are fixed on church gutters so water from the gutters comes out through the gargoyles' mouths.

Gaul   A person from an ancient region of Europe that covered the area of modern France and Belgium, as well as parts of Italy, Germany and the Netherlands.

gendarme   A member of the French police force that is part of the army.

Germanic   Of or relating to people who originally came from the regions of modern Scandinavia and Germany.

Gothic   Of or relating to a style of architecture that was popular in Europe from the mid-twelfth to the early sixteenth century.

Green   Belonging to a political party that is concerned with environmental issues, such as reducing pollution.

Greenwich Mean Time   The time in Greenwich, England, which stands on the zero line of longitude. It is used as a base for calculating the time in the rest of the world.

guillotine (noun)   A sharp metal blade set between two posts, used for cutting off people's heads.

guillotine (verb)   To behead with a guillotine.

Huguenot   A French Protestant. Most Huguenots believed in the ideas of the sixteenth-century Swiss religious leader John Calvin.

illegitimate   Born to unmarried parents.

immigrant   A person who comes to live in a country where he or she was not born and is not a citizen.

Impressionist   Of or belonging to the late nineteenth-century artistic movement known as Impressionism. Impressionist artists tried to paint scenes as they looked at a certain moment, for example, at dawn or dusk.

Indo-China   The regions of Southeast Asia between India and China that were once a French colony.

Industrial Revolution   The change from an agricultural to an industrial economy. In France, this revolution took place during the nineteenth century.

Joan of Arc   A young Frenchwoman who believed that God had chosen her to fight the English in the Hundred Years' War. She led the army that threw the English out of Orléans, but was finally captured and burned at the stake. She was made a saint in 1920.

Latin Quarter   The area on the Left Bank of the Seine where the University of Paris began and where the Sorbonne still stands. The Latin Quarter has long been a center for students, artists and intellectuals.

left-wing   Belonging to a political party that wants to make society better for ordinary people and the poor.

mausoleum   A place containing one or more large tombs where people, often the rich and famous, are buried.

Merovingian   Of or relating to the royal dynasty that ruled France from about 500 to 751 AD.

Nazi   A member of the National Socialist German Workers' Party, which was founded in 1919 and led by Adolf Hitler from 1921. The word is a short form of the German name for the party.

pasteurization   The process of heating cheese, milk and other foods and drinks to destroy harmful bacteria.

patron saint   A saint who is believed to protect and care for a particular place, organization or person.

persecution   Serious ill-treatment of people.

pogrom   An organized, violent attack, especially against Jews.

Prussia   A large North German state that went to war with France several times in the nineteenth century. Prussia was abolished after World War II.

rabies   A serious disease that can lead to death. Infected animals can pass it to humans by biting them.

Reign of Terror   The period from October 1793 to July 1794 when many opponents of the French Revolution were guillotined.

republic   A country or other political unit with elected rulers and no king or queen.

right-wing   Belonging to a political party that does not want to make dramatic changes or interfere in people's daily lives.

rose window   A circular window, often with ornamental stonework that divides it into a flowerlike shape.

suburb   A district on the edge of a city rather than in the center.

tagine   A stew of chicken or other meat that is often served with a semolinalike grain called couscous.

truffle   A rare type of edible fungus that grows underground.

tuberculosis   A serious, infectious disease that causes fever and often inflammation of the lungs.

Valois   Of or relating to the royal dynasty that ruled France from 1328 to 1589.

World War I   A major war that lasted from 1914 to 1918 and involved a large number of countries. Eventually France, Britain, Russia and the USA defeated Germany and Austria-Hungary.

World War II   A major war that lasted from 1939 to 1945 and involved a large number of countries. Eventually France, Britain, the USSR and the USA defeated Germany, Italy and Japan.

INDEX

Alphand, Adolphe 17
André Citroën Park 17
Arab World Institute 23
Arc de Triomphe 5, 6, 10, 31, 38, 45
arcades 30, 46
arrondissements 5, 6, 45
Art Nouveau 23, 28, 46
Arts Viaduct 42
Au Bon Marché 30

Bastille Day 38, 39, 43
Bastille Prison 10, 26, 27, 39, 45
Belleville 13, 19, 41
bicycle lanes 29, 43
Black Death 8
Bois de Boulogne 6, 17, 26, 35, 38, 39
Bois de Vincennes 6, 17, 23, 42
Botanical Garden 7, 17, 46
boules 16, 46
Boulevard Périphérique 4, 29
Bourbon dynasty 9, 44, 46
Bourbon Palace 5
Buddhists 23
Buttes-Chaumont Park 17

cabarets 35, 46
Capetian dynasty 8, 44
Carnavalet Museum 7, 36
Carolingian dynasty 8, 44, 46
Catholics 9, 22
cemeteries 16, 41
Chaillot 18
Chaillot Palace 6, 37, 42
Champs-Elysées, Avenue de 5, 6, 7, 34, 39
Charlemagne 8
Charles de Gaulle Bridge 7, 43
Charles VII, King 9
Châtelet Prison 26, 27
Chinatown 13, 38
Chirac, Jacques 11, 41, 43, 45
Cluny Museum 6, 7, 36
Comédie Française 6, 7, 34
Commune, the 11, 41, 45
Conciergerie 7, 27
Curie, Marie 15, 20

Curie, Pierre 20

Danton, Georges 26
De Gaulle, Charles 11, 43, 45
La Défense 25, 34
Delacroix Museum 6, 7, 37
Disneyland Paris 25, 35, 45
Dreyfus, Alfred 23

Edward III, King 9
Eiffel Tower 6, 15, 45
Elysée Palace 5, 6, 7
Enlightenment 9, 22
European Union 42, 46
Existentialists 32, 46

fashion 24, 25, 31
Forum des Halles 30
Francis I, King 9
Frankish kingdom 8, 46
French Institute 21
French Revolution 10, 11, 14, 15, 20, 26, 27, 36, 39, 45

Galeries Lafayette 30, 39
Garnier Opera House 4, 7, 15, 34
Gauls 8, 44, 46
Geneviève, Saint 40
La Grande Arche 6, 25
grandes écoles 20, 21, 41
Guimard Synagogue 23

Haussmann, Baron 10, 15, 18, 40, 45
Henry IV, King 9, 19
Hôtel des Invalides 6, 13, 44
Hôtel de Ville 5, 7
Hugo, Victor 14, 15, 40
Huguenots 9, 23, 44, 47
Hundred Years' War 9, 44

Ile de la Cité 4, 7, 14, 26, 27, 31
Ile de France region 4, 5
Ile St-Louis 4, 7, 18
immigrants 12, 47
Industrial Revolution 24, 47

Jews 13, 23

Joan of Arc 9, 47

Latin Quarter 4, 6, 7, 20, 21, 23, 26, 36, 47
Left Bank 4, 16, 17, 30, 31, 32
Longchamp racecourse 17, 39
Louis XIV, the Sun King 9, 14, 22, 27, 34, 44
Louis XV, King 9
Louis XVI, King 10
Louvre Museum 6, 7, 8, 24, 36, 42
Lutetia 8
Luxembourg Garden 6, 7, 16
Luxembourg Palace 5, 6, 7, 16
lycées 20, 21

Man in the Iron Mask, The 27
Marais 7, 18, 19
Marie Antoinette 10, 11, 27
Merovingian dynasty 8, 44, 47
Métro 28, 43, 45
Molière 34
Montmartre 7, 22, 26, 29, 31, 33, 35, 38, 39
Montparnasse 19, 32
Muslims 23

Napoleon Bonaparte (Emperor Napoleon I) 10, 14, 22, 27, 33, 45
Napoleon III, Emperor 10, 11, 16, 17, 45
National Library 6, 7, 15, 42
Nazis 11, 16, 23, 31, 45, 47
Notre-Dame Cathedral 4, 7, 8, 14, 22, 34, 39, 40, 44

Orsay Museum 6, 7, 36, 45

Palace of Versailles 9, 38
Palais d'Omnisports 7, 35, 42
Panthéon 6, 7, 15
Parc Astérix 35
Paris Mosque 7, 23
Parisii tribe 8
Pascal, Blaise 20
Pasteur, Louis 21, 41
Pepin the Short 8
Philip VI, King 9

Piaf, Edith 16, 41
Piano, Renzo 37, 42
Place de la Bastille 7
Place des Vosges 7, 19
police forces 26
Pompidou Centre 7, 15, 37, 42, 45
Printemps 30
Prix de l'Arc de Triomphe 39
Protestants 9, 22
Prussia 10, 11, 45, 47

racism 12
railroads 24, 28, 42
Reign of Terror 10, 27, 45, 47
Right Bank 4, 21, 30
Rogers, Richard 37

Sacré-Coeur church 7, 22, 29, 31, 45
St Bartholemew's Day Massacre 9, 44
Sainte-Chapelle 7, 22
La Samaritaine 30
Sartre, Jean-Paul 32
Science City 36, 37
Seine River 4, 6, 7, 8, 27, 29, 31, 43, 44
Sorbonne 6, 7, 20, 44
sport 35, 38, 39

theaters 34, 37, 39
Toulouse-Lautrec, Henri 35
Tuileries Garden 6, 7, 16

University of Paris 20, 21, 44, 45

Valois dynasty 9, 44, 47
Versailles, Palace of 14, 19, 3
Villette Park 17, 34, 35, 37
Voltaire 22, 27

Waiters' Race 38
Wars of Religion 9, 22, 44
World War I 11, 45, 46
World War II 11, 13, 16, 19, 23, 25, 45, 47

Zola, Emile 15, 23